40 minute
BIBLE STUDIES

D0342521

Spiritual Warfare: Overcoming the Enemy

Kay Arthur, David & BJ Lawson

PRECEPT MINISTRIES INTERNATIONAL

WATERBROOK
PRESS

Spiritual Warfare: Overcoming the Enemy
Published by WaterBrook Press
12265 Oracle Boulevard, Suite 200
Colorado Springs, Colorado 80921

All Scripture quotations are taken from the New American Standard Bible®. © Copyright
The Lockman Foundation 1960, 1962, 1963, 1968, 1971, 1972, 1973, 1975, 1977, 1995.
Used by permission. (www.Lockman.org).

Trade Paperback ISBN 978-0-307-72979-8
eBook ISBN 978-0-307-72980-4

Published in the United States by WaterBrook Multnomah, an imprint of the Crown
Publishing Group, a division of Random House LLC, New York, a Penguin Random House
Company.

Printed in the United States of America
2014

10 9 8 7

Special Sales
Most WaterBrook Multnomah books are available at special quantity discounts when
purchased in bulk by corporations, organizations, and special-interest groups. Custom
imprinting or excerpting can also be done to fit special needs. For information, please
e-mail SpecialMarkets@WaterBrookMultnomah.com or call 1-800-603-7051.

CONTENTS

HOW TO USE THIS STUDY

This small-group study is for people who are interested in learning for themselves more about what the Bible says on various subjects, but who have only limited time to meet together. It's ideal, for example, for a lunch group at work, an early morning men's group, a young mothers' group meeting in a home, a Sunday-school class, or even family devotions. (It's also ideal for small groups that typically have longer meeting times—such as evening groups or Saturday morning groups—but want to devote only a portion of their time together to actual study, while reserving the rest for prayer, fellowship, or other activities.)

This book is designed so that all the group's participants will complete each lesson's study activities *at the same time.* Discussing your insights drawn from what God says about the subject reveals exciting, life-impacting truths.

Although it's a group study, you'll need a facilitator to lead the study and keep the discussion moving. (This person's function is *not* that of a lecturer or teacher. However, when this book is used in a Sunday-school class or similar setting, the teacher should feel free to lead more directly and to bring in other insights in addition to those provided in each week's lesson.)

If *you* are your group's facilitator, the leader, here are some helpful points for making your job easier:

- Go through the lesson and mark the text before you lead the group. This will give you increased familiarity with the material and will enable you to facilitate the group with greater ease. It may be easier for you to lead the group through the instructions for marking if you, as a leader, choose a specific color for each symbol you mark.

- As you lead the group, start at the beginning of the text and simply read it aloud in the order it appears in the lesson, including the "insight boxes," which appear throughout. Work through the lesson together, observing and discussing what you learn. As you read the Scripture verses, have the group say aloud the word they are marking in the text.

- The discussion questions are there simply to help you cover the material. As the class moves into the discussion, many times you will find that they will cover the questions on their own. Remember, the discussion questions are there to guide the group through the topic, not to squelch discussion.

- Remember how important it is for people to verbalize their answers and discoveries. This greatly strengthens their personal understanding of each week's lesson. Try to ensure that everyone has plenty of opportunity to contribute to each week's discussions.

- Keep the discussion moving. This may mean spending more time on some parts of the study than on others. If necessary, you should feel free to spread out a lesson over more than one session. However, remember that you don't want to slow the pace too much. It's much better to leave everyone "wanting more" than to have people dropping out because of declining interest.

- If the validity or accuracy of some of the answers seems questionable, you can gently and cheerfully remind the group to stay focused on the truth of the Scriptures. Your object is to learn what the Bible says, not to engage in human philosophy. Simply stick with the Scriptures and give God the opportunity to speak. His Word *is* truth (John 17:17)!

SPIRITUAL WARFARE: OVERCOMING THE ENEMY

The first rule of battle is this: know your enemy. A thorough knowledge of the opponent's strength, his probable line of attack, and his tactics are vital to achieving victory. So how complete and accurate is your understanding of your enemy, the devil? Did you even know you had an enemy?

The Bible clearly shows that every one of us lives in the midst of a spiritual battle, whether or not we realize it. Yet many—even many believers—make the mistake of dismissing the enemy as a benign cartoon character with horns and a tail. Others become preoccupied with the enemy, fearfully focusing on his power rather than living in the reality of God's strength. As you'll discover in the weeks ahead, neither approach reflects the battle-ready perspective we need to walk daily in victory.

It is imperative that we have accurate information about our enemy, who is bent on destroying our ability to effectively serve God. For the next six weeks, you will dig into the Word of God to discover the truth about the devil for yourself. Knowing this truth will enable you to stand firm when you encounter the enemy!

Who is the devil? What do you know about him and where did you get your information? From movies? books? video games? As a follower of Christ, it is important that you know exactly who the devil is—because his goals involve you personally. The Bible has a lot to say about him, and this week we will begin to discover those truths for ourselves.

OBSERVE

We will begin our study in Genesis chapter 3. Keep in mind that the Bible is a progressive revelation of truth. In other words, God reveals truth little by little, building on what He has revealed before. We won't learn all there is to know about the devil in this lesson, but by the end of the course, you will be able to recognize him and his tactics.

Leader: Read Genesis 3:1–7 aloud.

  • *Have the group say aloud and mark each mention of **the serpent,** including pronouns, with a pitchfork, like this:* ⑊

GENESIS 3:1–7

¹ Now the serpent was more crafty than any beast of the field which the LORD God had made. And he said to the woman, "Indeed, has God said, 'You shall not eat from any tree of the garden'?"

² The woman said to the serpent, "From the fruit of the trees of the garden we may eat;

³ but from the fruit of the tree which is in the middle of the garden, God has said,

'You shall not eat from it or touch it, or you will die.' "

4 The serpent said to the woman, "You surely will not die!

5 "For God knows that in the day you eat from it your eyes will be opened, and you will be like God, knowing good and evil."

6 When the woman saw that the tree was good for food, and that it was a delight to the eyes, and that the tree was desirable to make one wise, she took from its fruit and ate; and she gave also to her husband with her, and he ate.

7 Then the eyes of both of them were

As you read the text, it's helpful to have the group say the key words aloud as they mark them. This way everyone will be sure they are marking every occurrence of the word, including any synonymous words or phrases. Do this throughout the study.

DISCUSS

• Look where you marked references to the serpent. What did you learn about the serpent, his character and his tactics?

• Discuss how the woman responded to the serpent and the action she took.

• What happened as a result of her actions?

OBSERVE

Eve ate the fruit and shared it with her husband. Their eyes were then opened, just as the serpent had promised. But the story doesn't end there.

Leader: *Read Genesis 3:8–13 aloud. Have the group say aloud and mark…*
  • *every mention of **LORD God**, including pronouns, with a triangle:* △
  • *each reference to **the serpent**, including pronouns, with a pitchfork.*

DISCUSS

• What did you learn about God in this passage?

---

opened, and they knew that they were naked; and they sewed fig leaves together and made themselves loin coverings.

GENESIS 3:8–13

8 They heard the sound of the LORD God walking in the garden in the cool of the day, and the man and his wife hid themselves from the presence of the LORD God among the trees of the garden.

9 Then the LORD God called to the man, and said to him, "Where are you?"

10 He said, "I heard the sound of You in the garden, and I was afraid because I was naked; so I hid myself."

11 And He said, "Who told you that you were naked? Have you eaten from the tree of which I commanded you not to eat?"

12 The man said, "The woman whom You gave to be with me, she gave me from the tree, and I ate."

13 Then the LORD God said to the woman, "What is this you have done?" And the woman said, "The serpent deceived me, and I ate."

• How did Adam and Eve respond to God, both in their behavior and conversation?

• What did you learn about the serpent and his tactics?

OBSERVE

God questioned the man and the woman. Then He turned His attention to the fourth participant in these events.

Leader: Read Genesis 3:14–15 aloud. Have the group say and mark…
- *every mention of LORD God, including pronouns, with a triangle.*
- *each reference to the serpent, including pronouns, with a pitchfork.*

DISCUSS

• Who was God speaking to in these verses, and what did He say?

• What did you learn about the serpent and his future?

• What did you learn about his ongoing relationship with mankind?

GENESIS 3:14–15

14 The LORD God said to the serpent, "Because you have done this, cursed are you more than all cattle, and more than every beast of the field; on your belly you will go, and dust you will eat all the days of your life;

15 and I will put enmity between you and the woman, and between your seed and her seed; he shall bruise you on the head, and you shall bruise him on the heel."

REVELATION 12:7–10

7 And there was war in heaven, Michael and his angels waging war with the dragon. The dragon and his angels waged war,

8 and they were not strong enough, and there was no longer a place found for them in heaven.

9 And the great dragon was thrown down, the serpent of old who is called the devil and Satan, who deceives the whole world; he was thrown down to the earth, and his angels were thrown down with him.

10 Then I heard a loud voice in heaven, saying, "Now the

OBSERVE

Now let's go to the last book of the Bible, where we'll learn the identity of the serpent. Revelation 12:7–10 describes a war in heaven. However, our focus today is not on the war but on learning more about the serpent, who plays a role in this war.

Leader: Read Revelation 12:7–10 aloud.

- *Have the group say aloud and mark with a pitchfork each reference to **the dragon,** including pronouns and synonyms. Watch carefully to be sure you mark all the names by which the dragon is called.*

DISCUSS

- What did you learn about the serpent?

- How is the serpent described? What name(s) is he called by?

• How does this compare to what you saw in Genesis 3?

• What are the serpent's tactics, according to verses 9 and 10?

salvation, and the power, and the kingdom of our God and the authority of His Christ have come, for the accuser of our brethren has been thrown down, he who accuses them before our God day and night."

• If the two passages you've looked at so far (Genesis 3:14–15 and Revelation 12:7–10) were your only sources of information about the enemy, what could you learn from them that applies to your own life?

OBSERVE

We've already gained vital knowledge about the enemy and his intentions, but the Bible provides much additional information about how the enemy works. To give His disciples insight on this topic, Jesus told a parable about a farmer who planted, or sowed, seed in his field. That night an enemy came and sowed weeds on the same soil. As a result, wheat and tares (weeds) grew up together. The farmer left the weeds alone until the harvest, knowing that in pulling out the tares he risked destroying the wheat. The disciples asked for an explanation and this is what Jesus said.

MATTHEW 13:37–39

Leader: Read Matthew 13:37–39 aloud.

> *• Have the group mark each reference to* ***the enemy,*** *including synonyms, with a pitchfork.*

37 And He said, "The one who sows the good seed is the Son of Man,

38 and the field is the world; and as for the good seed, these are the sons of the kingdom; and the tares are the sons of the evil one;

DISCUSS

• How is the enemy described?

• What has the enemy done?

39 and the enemy who sowed them is the devil, and the harvest is the end of the age; and the reapers are angels."

INSIGHT

The terms *Satan* and *the devil* both refer to a single entity—our enemy. *Satan* is found fifty-four times in the Old and New Testaments, while *devil* is used thirty-five times and occurs only in the New Testament.

Devil means "accuser, slanderer." *Satan* means "adversary, the enemy."

JOHN 8:44

You are of your father the devil, and you want to do the desires of your father. He was a murderer from the beginning, and does not stand in the truth because there is no truth in him. Whenever he speaks a lie, he speaks from his own nature, for he is a liar and the father of lies.

OBSERVE

In this next verse we find Jesus speaking to a group of religious leaders who refused to listen to the truth.

Leader: Read John 8:44 aloud.
  • *Have the group mark each reference to the devil, including pronouns, with a pitchfork.*

DISCUSS

• What did you learn about the devil? What words summarize his nature?

WRAP IT UP

Who is the devil? We've learned that he was the serpent in the garden with Eve in Genesis. He is also the great dragon who will one day be thrown down, according to Revelation 12. The devil also is known as Satan and the father of lies.

But the most important truth we discovered this week is that he is our enemy! From the beginning he has aligned himself against God and all who serve Him—and he will continue his fight to the end.

The devil is described in Genesis as being "more crafty than any beast of the field which the LORD God had made" (3:1). He questioned God's word, cast doubt over God's character, and deceived Eve into eating from the tree which God had said not to eat from. The devil was a murderer from the beginning, and there is no truth in him.

We can't afford to ignore the enemy or pretend he doesn't exist; but we also don't need to live in fear. God has equipped us with everything we need to defend ourselves against the devil's attacks. Determine today to finish all six weeks of this study so that you will recognize your enemy and his tactics.

We learned last week that we have an enemy who actively seeks our destruction. But how does he operate? What do we need to know about this enemy in order to stand in victory and not be caught off guard? These questions will be answered in this week's lesson.

OBSERVE

The devil is a dangerous enemy. What do Christians need to know in order to defeat him?

Leader: *Read 1 Peter 5:8 aloud.*

  • *Have the group say aloud and mark each reference to **the devil** with a pitch-fork:* ⑂

1 PETER 5:8

Be of sober spirit, be on the alert. Your adversary, the devil, prowls around like a roaring lion, seeking someone to devour.

DISCUSS

• How is the devil described?

• What does he do, and for what purpose?

2 Corinthians 2:10–11

10 But one whom
you forgive anything, I
[Paul] forgive also; for
indeed what I have
forgiven, if I have for-
given anything, I did it
for your sakes in the
presence of Christ,

11 so that no advan-
tage would be taken of
us by Satan, for we are
not ignorant of his
schemes.

Ephesians 6:11

Put on the full armor
of God, so that you
will be able to stand
firm against the
schemes of the devil.

OBSERVE

In the early church of Corinth, the believers were not willing to receive back into
their midst a man who had confessed his
sin and shown evidence of repentance for
his sin. These next two verses from
2 Corinthians reveal the apostle Paul's
response to the situation. (We will see the
context of Ephesians 6:11 later in our
study.)

*Leader: Read 2 Corinthians 2:10–11 and
Ephesians 6:11 aloud. Have the group say
aloud and…*

- *mark each reference to **Satan** or **the
  devil**, including pronouns, with a
  pitchfork.*
- *draw a box around each occurrence of
  the word **schemes:***

DISCUSS

- What did you learn about Satan and his
  schemes from these verses?

OBSERVE

Jesus gave us a clear example of what it means to be aware of and prepared for the devil's schemes.

Leader: *Read Matthew 4:1–4 aloud. Have the group do the following:*
- *Mark every reference to **Jesus,** including pronouns, with a cross:* †
- *Mark each reference to **the devil** or **the tempter** with a pitchfork.*
- *Underline the phrase **it is written.***

DISCUSS

- What did you learn about Jesus in these verses?

- What did you learn about the devil and his tactics?

1 Then Jesus was led up by the Spirit into the wilderness to be tempted by the devil.

2 And after He had fasted forty days and forty nights, He then became hungry.

3 And the tempter came and said to Him, "If You are the Son of God, command that these stones become bread."

4 But He answered and said, "It is written, 'Man shall not live on bread alone, but on every word that proceeds out of the mouth of God.' "

• What was the devil trying to persuade Jesus to do?

• How did Jesus respond to the devil's tempting?

MATTHEW 4:5–7

⁵ Then the devil took Him into the holy city and had Him stand on the pinnacle of the temple,

⁶ and said to Him, "If You are the Son of God, throw Yourself down; for it is written,

OBSERVE

The devil's first effort to tempt Jesus failed, but that did not keep him from trying again.

Leader: Read Matthew 4:5–7 aloud. Have the group do the following:
- *Mark each reference to **the devil,** including pronouns, with a pitchfork.*
- *Mark every reference to **Jesus,** including pronouns, with a cross.*
- *Underline the phrase **it is written.***

DISCUSS

• What did you learn about Satan and his tactics in this passage?

• What subtle difference did you notice in the devil's tactics in this second temptation? (Hint: look where you underlined ___it is written___).

• Why did the devil take Jesus to the pinnacle of the temple?

• How did Jesus respond to this temptation?

'He will command His angels concerning You'; and 'On their hands they will bear You up, so that You will not strike Your foot against a stone.' "

⁷ Jesus said to him, "On the other hand, it is written, 'You shall not put the Lord your God to the test.' "

MATTHEW 4:8-11

8 Again, the devil took Him to a very high mountain and showed Him all the kingdoms of the world and their glory;

9 and he said to Him, "All these things I will give You, if You fall down and worship me."

10 Then Jesus said to him, "Go, Satan! For it is written, 'You shall worship the Lord your God, and serve Him only.' "

11 Then the devil left Him; and behold, angels came and began to minister to Him.

OBSERVE

Let's consider the devil's third and final attempt in the wilderness to tempt Jesus to walk independently of God.

Leader: Read Matthew 4:8–11 aloud. Have the group do the following:
- *Mark each reference to **the devil,** including pronouns, with a pitchfork.*
- *Mark every reference to **Jesus,** including pronouns, with a cross:* †
- *Underline the phrase **it is written.***

DISCUSS

- What did you learn from these verses about the devil and his tactics?

- Once again, how did Jesus respond?

- If Jesus had given in to this particular temptation, how would it have affected God's plan for salvation?

• As we saw at the start of the lesson, we are to be on the alert because our adversary the devil is seeking someone to devour (1 Peter 5:8). Discuss what you have learned so far about the tactics and schemes of the devil.

• Have you ever been tempted in any of the areas of life where Satan targeted Jesus? How did you handle it?

• Jesus provided a great example for us to follow as He was tempted by the devil. How can we apply in our own lives what we've learned from Him?

• What is the greatest weapon you have against your adversary?

• Will it be enough to simply know the enemy's tactics? What else do you need to know? Explain your answer.

WRAP IT UP

Did you notice how the devil's temptations of Jesus in the wilderness were similar to his tactics with Eve in the garden?

In each case Satan altered God's words, twisting them in an effort to confuse and deceive. In each situation, he also appealed to the physical appetite, personal gain, and desire for power. Today Satan, the prince of this world, often tempts people in the same three categories. That's why we need to keep in mind this reality:

> For all that is in the world, the lust of the flesh and the lust of the eyes and the boastful pride of life, is not from the Father, but is from the world. The world is passing away, and also its lusts; but the one who does the will of God lives forever. (1 John 2:16–17)

We must be on the alert! Our enemy, the devil, is seeking to devour us. He is subtle and scheming and skilled in the art of temptation. The word *schemes*, which we saw used in connection with his tactics, carries the idea of cleverness, crafty methods, cunning, and deception. That is why we must be alert and not be caught off guard. Ask God to keep your spiritual senses sharp and your eyes open to the enemy's schemes.

Father, please keep us alert and aware of the enemy's tactics so that we would not be caught off guard. Teach us to stand firm in Your truth in our own lives and intercede in prayer as we see Satan attacking others.

Wars usually involve nations, kingdoms, or some sort of political entities fighting one another for control of people and territory. But Scripture describes an ongoing heavenly, or spiritual, battle. Two kingdoms are at war, and you, friend, belong to one of them. Whose side are you on?

OBSERVE

In Acts 26 we find the apostle Paul describing the encounter on the road to Damascus that led to his believing in Jesus as the Messiah. Let's look at the verses where he relates the words Jesus spoke to him.

Leader: Read Acts 26:16–18 aloud. Have the group say aloud and...

- *draw a box around the word **dominion:***
- *mark the reference to **Satan** with a pitchfork*

DISCUSS

- What dominions did you find mentioned in these verses?

ACTS 26:16–18

16 But get up and stand on your feet; for this purpose I have appeared to you, to appoint you a minister and a witness not only to the things which you have seen, but also to the things in which I will appear to you;

17 rescuing you from the Jewish people and from the Gentiles, to whom I am sending you,

18 to open their eyes so that they may turn from darkness to light and

from the dominion of Satan to God, that they may receive forgiveness of sins and an inheritance among those who have been sanctified by faith in Me.

• What did you learn about each?

• How does a person move from Satan's dominion to God's?

• What do those who turn to God receive?

OBSERVE

Colossians is a letter from the apostle Paul to the church at Colossae. In chapter 1 he described what God did for us when we came to faith in Christ.

COLOSSIANS 1:13–14

13 For He [God] rescued us from the domain of darkness, and transferred us to the kingdom of His beloved Son,

14 in whom we have redemption, the forgiveness of sins.

Leader: Read Colossians 1:13–14 aloud. Have the group say aloud and...
- *mark all pronouns that refer to **God** with a triangle:* △
- *draw a box around the words **domain** and **kingdom.***

DISCUSS
• What did God do?

• What are the characteristics of the two domains, or kingdoms, described in verse 13?

OBSERVE

Ephesians 2:1–3 details the spiritual condition of the believer before being transferred by God to the kingdom of His beloved Son.

Leader: Read Ephesians 2:1–3 aloud. Have the group do the following:
  • *Circle all personal pronouns:* **you, your, we,** *and* **our.**
  • *Mark the word* **prince** *with a pitchfork.*
  • *Underline the phrases* **according to** *and* **working in.**

DISCUSS

• What did you learn from marking all the personal pronouns?

EPHESIANS 2:1–3

1 And you were dead in your trespasses and sins,

2 in which you formerly walked according to the course of this world, according to the prince of the power of the air, of the spirit that is now working in the sons of disobedience.

3 Among them we too all formerly lived in the lusts of our flesh, indulging the desires of the flesh and of the mind, and were by nature children of wrath, even as the rest.

• Who do you think is the prince mentioned in verse 2? Explain your answer.

• How is he described?

• Where does he work?

• What was our relationship to him before we moved into the kingdom of God?

---

11 Put on the full armor of God, so that you will be able to stand firm against the schemes of the devil.

12 For our struggle is not against flesh and blood, but against the

OBSERVE

As members of God's kingdom, we remain at war with an unseen but very treacherous enemy.

Leader: *Read Ephesians 6:11–12 aloud. Have the group…*
  • *mark the word **devil** with a pitchfork.*
  • *draw a squiggly line like this* ⌇⌇⌇ *under the word **struggle**.*

DISCUSS

• What did you learn about the devil?

rulers, against the powers, against the world forces of this darkness, against the spiritual forces of wickedness in the heavenly places.

• Who is our spiritual struggle with?

• Where does this struggle take place? Explain your answer.

• What evidence have you seen of the devil's schemes against believers?

1 JOHN 3:7–10

7 Little children, make sure no one deceives you; the one who practices righteousness is righteous, just as He [Jesus] is righteous;

8 the one who practices sin is of the devil; for the devil has sinned from the beginning. The Son of God appeared for this purpose, to destroy the works of the devil.

9 No one who is born of God practices sin, because His seed abides in him; and he cannot sin, because he is born of God.

10 By this the children of God and the children of the devil

OBSERVE

A group of false teachers in the early church taught that knowledge—what a person believed—was all that mattered, so the way an individual lived was unimportant. To counteract this lie, the apostle John taught his disciples that how we live reveals who our father is.

Leader: Read 1 John 3:7–10 aloud. Have the group say and…
- *mark each reference to **the devil** with a pitchfork.*
- *draw a box around each occurrence of the word **practices** and the phrase **does not practice.***

DISCUSS

• What are the characteristics of the children of God? What is their practice, their lifestyle?

• By contrast, what are the distinctive characteristics of the children of the devil?

INSIGHT

The verb tenses in 1 John 3 help clarify the distinctions between the children of God and the children of the devil. The Greek word translated as *practices* in this passage is a present-tense verb, implying continuous or habitual action—a pattern of behavior or a lifestyle.

are obvious: anyone who does not practice righteousness is not of God, nor the one who does not love his brother.

• According to verse 8, what was the purpose for which Jesus, the Son of God, came?

• What does this tell you about our spiritual battle?

HEBREWS 2:14–15

14 Therefore, since the children share in flesh and blood, He Himself [Jesus] likewise also partook of the same, that through death He might render powerless him who had the power of death, that is, the devil,

15 and might free those who through fear of death were subject to slavery all their lives.

OBSERVE

As we've seen, before God rescued us we were captives to the domain of darkness. Let's consider how our situation has changed as a result of that rescue.

Leader: Read Hebrews 2:14–15 aloud. Have the group say aloud and mark...

- *the pronouns **He** and **Himself**, which refer to **Jesus**, with a cross:* †
- *each reference to **the devil**, including pronouns, with a pitchfork.*

DISCUSS

- What did Jesus do, and how did He do it?

- What effect did Jesus's actions have on the devil's power?

- So we don't miss it, Romans 6:23 says, "The wages of sin is death." Now stop and think. It is sin that gives the devil the power of death. So how did Jesus take away that power?

OBSERVE

Let's look at one more verse that describes how moving into the kingdom of God sets us free.

1 JOHN 5:19

We know that we are of God, and that the whole world lies in the power of the evil one.

Leader: Read 1 John 5:19 aloud. Have the group…
- *mark **evil one** with a pitchfork.*
- *circle each occurrence of the word (**we**,) which in this verse refers to **believers.***

DISCUSS

• Who lies in the power of the evil one?

• Based on all you've learned in this lesson, which kingdom are you in?

• Do you lie in the power of the evil one?

• How do you know?

WRAP IT UP

This week we learned that two kingdoms are at war: the kingdom of the devil and the kingdom of God. One is a kingdom of darkness while the other is a kingdom of light. If you are a believer, you have been rescued by God from the kingdom of darkness and have been transferred into the kingdom of His beloved Son. You once were ruled by the one who has sinned from the beginning. But now you are ruled by the One who offers forgiveness of sin.

Unbelievers live in the flesh—the kingdom of darkness—and are ruled by the devil. Therefore, sin is their practice, their way of life. But believers are no longer slaves to sin and Satan. We have forgiveness of sin through the blood of Jesus Christ, which means the devil's grip on us has been broken. In freedom, we now serve a new king and the habit of our lives will be to walk in righteousness (1 John 3:7–10).

Although Jesus came to destroy the works of the enemy, He didn't annihilate Satan. The enemy is certainly alive and well today. However, Jesus has taken away his power over us by making the payment for our sin. While Satan is still powerful, he is no match for almighty God. He is a defeated enemy! Satan may win a battle here and there, but he has already lost the war. It is written in God's book (Revelation 20:10).

Do not be deceived! It is obvious by one's life which kingdom one belongs to. Examine yourself to be sure of which king you are serving.

Father, would You enable us to honestly examine our lives? Please show us clearly whose kingdom we belong to.

In the previous three lessons, you have seen that you have an enemy. This is war! Have you ever wondered if Satan is free to carry out his plans and attacks on whomever, wherever, and whenever he wants? Does God have any influence over the devil's schemes—does He even know it is happening? Do Satan and God have an equal balance of power?

This week we will find the answers to these questions and more.

OBSERVE

The story of Job gives us insights into Satan's strategy and the scope of his power. But before we learn more about our enemy, let's first take a look at the man Job.

Leader: Read Job 1:1–5 aloud.

- *Have the group say aloud and mark every reference to **Job,** including synonyms and pronouns, with a **J.***

DISCUSS

- How is Job's character described in verse 1?

JOB 1:1–5

¹ There was a man in the land of Uz whose name was Job; and that man was blameless, upright, fearing God and turning away from evil.

² Seven sons and three daughters were born to him.

³ His possessions also were 7,000 sheep, 3,000 camels, 500 yoke of oxen, 500 female donkeys, and very many servants;

and that man was the greatest of all the men of the east.

4 His sons used to go and hold a feast in the house of each one on his day, and they would send and invite their three sisters to eat and drink with them.

5 When the days of feasting had completed their cycle, Job would send and consecrate them, rising up early in the morning and offering burnt offerings according to the number of them all; for Job said, "Perhaps my sons have sinned and cursed God in their hearts." Thus Job did continually.

• What did you learn about Job as a person in this passage?

• What was his relationship to God? His status in his community?

OBSERVE

Now that we have met Job, the author of this book of the Bible introduces us to the adversary. Let's see what the book of Job has to show us about Satan's character, his work, his limitations, and his relationship to God.

Leader: Read Job 1:6–12 aloud. Have the group say and mark…
- *every reference to **the Lord,** including pronouns, with a triangle:* △
- *each reference to **Satan,** including pronouns, with a pitchfork* ⚡

DISCUSS

• What did you learn about Satan in this passage?

• What does the fact that Satan is *roaming about on the earth* imply about his awareness of and relationship to man?

JOB 1:6–12

6 Now there was a day when the sons of God came to present themselves before the LORD, and Satan also came among them.

7 The LORD said to Satan, "From where do you come?" Then Satan answered the LORD and said, "From roaming about on the earth and walking around on it."

8 The LORD said to Satan, "Have you considered My servant Job? For there is no one like him on the earth, a blameless and upright man, fearing God and turning away from evil."

9 Then Satan answered the LORD, "Does Job fear God for nothing?

10 "Have You not made a hedge about him and his house and all that he has, on every side? You have blessed the work of his hands, and his possessions have increased in the land.

11 "But put forth Your hand now and touch all that he has; he will surely curse You to Your face."

12 Then the LORD said to Satan, "Behold, all that he has is in your power, only do not put forth your hand on him." So Satan departed from the presence of the LORD.

• What did God bring to Satan's attention?

• What did God say about Job? How does that relate to what we saw in verses 1–5?

• In these verses what did Satan suggest was Job's motive for serving God?

• How do you suppose Satan knew there was a hedge about Job?

• What does that show you about God's power?

• Could Satan do whatever he wanted with Job? Explain your answer.

OBSERVE

With the stage set, let's take a look at Satan's first attack on Job.

Leader: Read Job 1:13–22 aloud. Have the group…
- mark every reference to **Job,** including synonyms and pronouns, with a **J.**
- number each of the attacks on Job's family. The first one is numbered for you.

DISCUSS

- Summarize the various ways Satan attacked Job.

- What do these attacks show about Satan's power?

JOB 1:13–22

13 Now on the day when his sons and his daughters were eating and drinking wine in their oldest brother's house,

14 a messenger came to Job and said, "The oxen were plowing and the donkeys feeding beside them,

15 and the ①Sabeans attacked and took them. They also slew the servants with the edge of the sword, and I alone have escaped to tell you."

16 While he was still speaking, another also came and said, "The fire of God fell from heaven and burned up the sheep and the

servants and consumed them, and I alone have escaped to tell you."

17 While he was still speaking, another also came and said, "The Chaldeans formed three bands and made a raid on the camels and took them and slew the servants with the edge of the sword, and I alone have escaped to tell you."

18 While he was still speaking, another also came and said, "Your sons and your daughters were eating and drinking wine in their oldest brother's house,

19 and behold, a great wind came from across the wilderness and struck the four corners

• According to verse 20, how did Job respond to Satan's assault?

• Did Job respond as Satan had predicted he would? Explain your answer.

• Why would Job, or someone like him, be a target for Satan?

• Discuss what you've learned in Job chapter 1 about both God and Satan. How might those lessons apply to us today?

of the house, and it fell on the young people and they died, and I alone have escaped to tell you."

20 Then Job arose and tore his robe and shaved his head, and he fell to the ground and worshiped.

21 He said, "Naked I came from my mother's womb, And naked I shall return there. The LORD gave and the LORD has taken away. Blessed be the name of the LORD."

22 Through all this Job did not sin nor did he blame God.

JOB 2:1–10

¹ Again there was a day when the sons of God came to present themselves before the LORD, and Satan also came among them to present himself before the LORD.

² The LORD said to Satan, "Where have you come from?" Then Satan answered the LORD and said, "From roaming about on the earth and walking around on it."

³ The LORD said to Satan, "Have you considered My servant Job? For there is no one like him on the earth, a blameless and upright man fearing God and turning away from evil. And he still

OBSERVE

Despite these tragedies, Job did not compromise his faith. He stood firm. However, Satan wasn't finished.

Leader: Read Job 2:1–10 aloud. Have the group say and mark…
- *every reference to **the Lord**, including pronouns, with a triangle.*
- *each reference to **Satan**, including pronouns, with a pitchfork.*

DISCUSS

- What did you learn about Job in this passage?

- Who brought up Job this time, and how was he described?

• The contest was about to get even more intense. What did Satan ask God for permission to do?

• How did Job's wife respond to the new challenge?

• Have you ever endured similar pressure from a loved one while in a trial? If so, what did you do?

• How did Job respond? Did he lose his integrity?

• From what you have seen so far, what is the extent of God's sovereignty? In other words, what does He have authority or power over?

holds fast his integrity, although you incited Me against him to ruin him without cause."

4 Satan answered the LORD and said, "Skin for skin! Yes, all that a man has he will give for his life.

5 "However, put forth Your hand now, and touch his bone and his flesh; he will curse You to Your face."

6 So the LORD said to Satan, "Behold, he is in your power, only spare his life."

7 Then Satan went out from the presence of the LORD and smote Job with sore boils from the sole of

his foot to the crown of his head.

8 And he took a potsherd to scrape himself while he was sitting among the ashes.

9 Then his wife said to him, "Do you still hold fast your integrity? Curse God and die!"

10 But he said to her, "You speak as one of the foolish women speaks. Shall we indeed accept good from God and not accept adversity?" In all this Job did not sin with his lips.

• If Satan were to stand before the Lord right now, would your character be such that God would boast of you to him? Explain your answer.

• If Satan were to challenge your motives for serving God, would God express the same confidence in you? Why or why not?

• When the enemy assaults you with trials, testing, and tragedies, what lessons from Job's life can you apply to yours?

WRAP IT UP

From Job's story we have learned that Satan roams about the earth and he is aware of what's happening where we live. He knows who is truly living for God, and he targets those individuals as a threat to his kingdom.

But God, too, is quite aware of what's happening on earth. It was God who brought Job to the attention of Satan, pointing out his virtues: "a blameless and upright man, fearing God and turning away from evil" (Job 1:8).

Satan responded with a complaint: "Have You not made a hedge about him and his house and all that he has, on every side? You have blessed the work of his hands, and his possessions have increased in the land" (Job 1:10). Satan knew there was a hedge around Job because he obviously couldn't get to him without God's permission! How comforting that ought to be to us. Did you realize God can put hedges about us to protect us from the attacks of our adversary?

Satan not only complained about the limits placed on his power, but he also challenged God's evaluation of His servant. He accused Job of serving God only because he'd been so richly blessed. Then Satan threw down the gauntlet: "But put forth Your hand now and touch all that he has; he will surely curse You to Your face" (Job 1:11).

You'll notice Satan didn't brag that he would do anything he pleased to Job! Why? Because his power is limited by God. It always has been, and it always will be. The enemy can't do a thing without God's permission. (See Ephesians 1:20–23; Daniel 4:34–35.)

If Job could withstand the onslaught of Satan's attacks, how much more should you and I be able to do the same? We have the power of the Holy Spirit living in us. When you are tempted by the evil one, don't faint! Determine to stand firm. Remember, "the LORD has established His throne in the heavens, and His sovereignty rules over all" (Psalm 103:19).

Satan's primary objective is to get us into sin, to persuade us to walk independently of God. His primary tactic is to target our minds. Why? Because our thoughts determine our actions.

What do you think about? How can you cooperate with Jesus in order to win the battle for your mind? This week's lesson will give you much food for thought.

OBSERVE

Let's look together at some passages that reveal why the mind is the primary battlefield in spiritual warfare.

By the way, in these passages the word *heart* is synonymous with *mind.*

Leader: *Read aloud Proverbs 4:23; 15:28; Isaiah 26:3; and Matthew 15:18–19.*

- *Have the group say aloud and mark every occurrence of the words **heart** and **mind** with a heart:* ♡

DISCUSS

- What did you learn about the heart, or mind, from these verses?

PROVERBS 4:23

Watch over your heart with all diligence, for from it flow the springs of life.

PROVERBS 15:28

The heart of the righteous ponders how to answer, but the mouth of the wicked pours out evil things.

ISAIAH 26:3

The steadfast of mind You will keep in perfect peace, because he trusts in You.

MATTHEW 15:18–19

18 But the things that proceed out of the mouth come from the heart, and those defile the man.

19 For out of the heart come evil thoughts, murders, adulteries, fornications, thefts, false witness, slanders.

ACTS 5:3

But Peter said, "Ananias, why has Satan filled your heart to lie to the Holy Spirit and to keep back some of the price of the land?"

• What is the relationship between your mind and how you speak, think, or act?

• According to Isaiah 26:3, what is the relationship between a steadfast mind, perfect peace, and trust? How can we experience perfect peace?

• What does Matthew 15:18–19 show you about the connection between thoughts and actions? Where are a person's actions rooted?

OBSERVE

Let's look at the following verses and see how Satan targets the mind (heart) to accomplish his purposes.

Leader: Read aloud Acts 5:3; 2 Corinthians 11:3; and 4:3–4. Have the group…
- *mark each reference to **Satan,** including synonyms, with a pitchfork.*
- *draw a heart over the words **heart** and **minds.***

DISCUSS

• Discuss each of these verses. Note specifically who is influencing whom and what results from that influence.

• From what you've read so far, why would the mind be a primary target of the enemy?

2 CORINTHIANS 11:3

But I am afraid that, as the serpent deceived Eve by his craftiness, your minds will be led astray from the simplicity and purity of devotion to Christ.

2 CORINTHIANS 4:3–4

3 And even if our gospel is veiled, it is veiled to those who are perishing,

4 in whose case the god of this world has blinded the minds of the unbelieving so that they might not see the light of the gospel of the glory of Christ, who is the image of God.

2 CORINTHIANS 10:3–6

3 For though we walk in the flesh, we do not war according to the flesh,

4 for the weapons of our warfare are not of the flesh, but divinely powerful for the destruction of fortresses.

5 We are destroying speculations and every lofty thing raised up against the knowledge of God, and we are taking every thought captive to the obedience of Christ,

6 and we are ready to punish all disobedience, whenever your obedience is complete.

OBSERVE

Since the mind is a key battleground in spiritual warfare, how does a believer combat wrong thinking? The apostle Paul set forth some principles for defending our minds against the enemy.

Leader: Read 2 Corinthians 10:3–6 aloud. Have the group...
- *draw a circle around the words (we) and our, which in this passage refer to believers.*
- *underline the word __war__ and the phrase __weapons of our warfare.__*

DISCUSS

- What did you learn about believers in this passage?

- What principles of defense are described in this passage?

- What did you learn about Paul's example? What was he doing with his thoughts?

• Verse 3 says, "We do not war according to the flesh." So how are spiritual battles to be fought?

• What type of thoughts need to be destroyed?

• What exactly was Paul taking captive to the obedience of Christ?

• Discuss some examples of wrong thinking that might affect us.

• When these thoughts come, how should they be handled?

• From what you have seen so far, what might happen if we dwell on untrue thoughts instead of focusing on the truth of Christ?

OBSERVE

You may be asking, how do we know what thoughts are good and which are bad? When a thought comes, how can you know whether to welcome it or destroy it?

PHILIPPIANS 4:8–9

8 Finally, brethren, whatever① is true, whatever is honorable, whatever is right, whatever is pure, whatever is lovely, whatever is of good repute, if there is any excellence and if anything worthy of praise, dwell on these things.

9 The things you have learned and received and heard and seen in me, practice these things, and the God of peace will be with you.

Leader: Read Philippians 4:8–9 aloud.
- *Number each **whatever** in the text. The first one is numbered for you.*
- *Underline the phrase **dwell on these things.***

DISCUSS

- What exactly did Paul teach the Philippians to do in these verses?

- What things are we to dwell on, to focus our minds on?

• How do these verses compare with what you just saw in 2 Corinthians 10:5?

• What do you do when thoughts come to mind that are contrary to this list?

• Our thought life is influenced by a variety of outside sources such as conversations, books, movies, the Internet, television, friendships, and music. How does the counsel of Philippians 4:8 relate to these influences in your life?

WRAP IT UP

What happens when an ungodly thought goes unchecked? The thought can lead to an action. If it is repeated enough, it becomes a habit. Eventually it can become a base of oppression for the enemy—what some call a stronghold, or what Paul, in 2 Corinthians 10:4, called a fortress.

These strongholds of wrong thinking need to be torn down, destroyed. Any speculation (imagination) or thinking that is contrary to God, to His Word, and to our position in Christ and what God says about us is to be destroyed. We are not to allow these thoughts to continue. If we do, Satan will achieve a victory in our lives. Any thought that would lead us to disobedience or unbelief is not from God, and it, too, must be dealt with.

Our strategy for winning the battle of the mind is made clear in Paul's example. "We are taking every thought captive to the obedience of Christ" (2 Corinthians 10:5). This is not simply a one-time action; it is a continual process. Moment by moment, we must evaluate our thoughts and bring our minds under control.

Is there anything you feel compelled to dwell on—to think about—even though you know it does not meet the standards of Philippians 4:8? If so, it's a stronghold—and it needs to be destroyed before the enemy gains a further advantage.

Next week we'll look at other strategies for resisting the devil. For today, spend some time evaluating your thought life. Since wrong thinking is one of Satan's tactics, in what areas do you need to build up your defenses or tear down strongholds?

As important as it is to be aware of our enemy's battle tactics, the most vital truth to remember is this: *we win!* Or more accurately, Christ has already won, and we get to live in His victory. The enemy is dangerous, but Christ is victorious. You're going to enjoy learning more about these truths this week.

OBSERVE

In his letter to the Ephesians, the apostle Paul gave thanks for their faith and described how he was praying for these believers.

Leader: Read Ephesians 1:18–23 aloud. Have the group say aloud and mark...

- *every reference to **Jesus**, including pronouns, with a cross:* †
- *each occurrence of the words **power** and **might** with a* **P.**

DISCUSS

- From what you saw in verses 18–19, what was Paul's prayer for the believers? Why?

EPHESIANS 1:18–23

18 I pray that the eyes of your heart may be enlightened, so that you will know what is the hope of His [God's] calling, what are the riches of the glory of His inheritance in the saints,

19 and what is the surpassing greatness of His power toward us who believe. These are in accordance with the working of the strength of His might

20 which He brought about in Christ, when

He raised Him from the dead and seated Him at His right hand in the heavenly places,

21 far above all rule and authority and power and dominion, and every name that is named, not only in this age but also in the one to come.

22 And He put all things in subjection under His feet, and gave Him [Jesus] as head over all things to the church,

23 which is His body, the fullness of Him who fills all in all.

• What did you learn about the power mentioned here, especially as it relates to God the Father and Christ?

• What relevance does their power have for our lives?

• Is any authority or power, human or in the spirit realm, greater than Jesus? Explain your answer.

• Is any created thing or being equal to God?

• You have already seen that Satan is a created being. So, is he God's equal? Explain your answer.

• Practically speaking, what does this mean for believers?

OBSERVE

Throughout the Bible God instructs us about the enemy and how to prepare for our encounters with him. In Ephesians we find further counsel so that we will not be caught off guard but will be able to stand in victory.

Leader: *Read Ephesians 6:10–13 aloud. Have the group do the following:*
- *underline **each instruction** given by Paul.*
- *draw a box around the phrase **stand firm:*** ☐
- *draw a pitchfork over every reference to **the devil** and **those under his power or associated with him:*** ⑁

DISCUSS

- What instructions did Paul give to the Ephesians?

- What would be accomplished by their following these instructions?

EPHESIANS 6:10–13

10 Finally, be strong in the Lord and in the strength of His might.

11 Put on the full armor of God, so that you will be able to stand firm against the schemes of the devil.

12 For our struggle is not against flesh and blood, but against the rulers, against the powers, against the world forces of this darkness, against the spiritual forces of wickedness in the heavenly places.

13 Therefore, take up the full armor of God, so that you will be able

to resist in the evil day, and having done every-thing, to stand firm.

• According to these verses, is the devil alone in his battle against us?

• Who are our enemies? Where is our struggle?

INSIGHT

The Greek word translated here as *struggle* speaks of *wrestling* or *hand-to-hand combat*. It indicates hard, dangerous, up-close fighting.

• Where are our spiritual enemies located, and why does that make them even more dangerous?

• So when you are being persecuted, who is your enemy?

• Are these attacks personal or spiritual?

• How will identifying your true enemy help when you are being persecuted?

• What is it that enables a believer to stand firm against the devil?

• Whose armor are we given, and why is it vital to our struggle?

EPHESIANS 6:14–17

14 Stand firm therefore, having girded your loins with truth, and having put on the breastplate of righteousness,

15 and having shod your feet with the preparation of the gospel of peace;

16 in addition to all, taking up the shield of faith with which you will be able to extinguish all the flaming arrows of the evil one.

17 And take the helmet of salvation, and the sword of the Spirit, which is the word of God.

OBSERVE

Since we are fighting enemies in the spirit world, we need special equipment—and God has provided it for us.

Leader: Read Ephesians 6:14–17 aloud. Have the group say and…
- *draw a box around the phrase **stand firm.***
- *mark the phrase **the evil one** with a pitchfork.*

DISCUSS

- What command did you find in verse 14?

- In order to stand firm against the enemy, what is the believer to do?

- Discuss the purpose or function of each of the things we are to put on.

• Specifically, what does the shield of faith enable a believer to do?

• What are the last two pieces of armor we are told to take up?

• How is the sword of the Spirit described?

• Discuss these last two pieces and why they are important in our encounters with the enemy.

EPHESIANS 6:18–20

¹⁸ With all prayer and petition pray at all times in the Spirit, and with this in view, be on the alert with all perseverance and petition for all the saints,

¹⁹ and pray on my behalf, that utterance may be given to me in the opening of my mouth, to make known with boldness the mystery of the gospel,

²⁰ for which I am an ambassador in chains; that in proclaiming it I may speak boldly, as I ought to speak.

OBSERVE

Having put on the full armor of God, what other defense tactics will help you stand firm?

Leader: Read Ephesians 6:18–20 aloud. Have the group...
- *mark the words **prayer, petition,** and **pray** with a **P.***
- *underline **each command.***

DISCUSS

- What did you learn about prayer in these verses?

INSIGHT

Prayer in general implies speaking to God, which includes asking.

Petition is speaking to God with a specific request in mind.

• What does it mean to pray in the Spirit?

• What does praying in the Spirit have to do with war?

• Who are we to be praying for? Why?

• What was mentioned in this text that you can petition God for?

• Even Paul asked for prayer. What were his circumstances, according to verse 20?

• How did he want the Ephesians to pray for him? Why?

• If even the apostle Paul asked for prayer, what does this suggest about our own need for prayer in the face of spiritual warfare?

• Have you ever felt as if you couldn't withstand the bombardment of temptations thrown your way? Do you wonder if you are strong enough to survive the attack?

• From what you have seen, how can we as believers stand firm, no matter what the devil throws at us?

1 PETER 5:8–9

8 Be of sober spirit, be on the alert. Your adversary, the devil, prowls around like a roaring lion, seeking someone to devour.

9 But resist him, firm in your faith, knowing that the same experiences of suffering are

OBSERVE

As believers we are to trust the Lord. However, that doesn't mean we need to be casual about the spiritual battle taking place around us. God has already won the victory, but we have responsibilities as well.

Leader: Read 1 Peter 5:8–9 aloud. Have the group...

• *underline **each instruction.***

• *mark every reference to **the devil**, including pronouns, with a pitchfork.*

DISCUSS

• What does the devil do? What is his goal?

• How are we to respond to the devil?

OBSERVE

Is it possible to overcome the evil one?

Leader: *Read 1 John 2:13–14 aloud. Have the group say aloud and...*
  • *mark each occurrence of the word **overcome** with an **O**.*
  • *draw a pitchfork over each reference to **the evil one**.*

DISCUSS

• What is the connection between the Word of God and those who overcome the devil?

---

being accomplished by your brethren who are in the world.

1 JOHN 2:13–14

13 I am writing to you, fathers, because you know Him who has been from the beginning. I am writing to you, young men, because you have overcome the evil one. I have written to you, children, because you know the Father.

14 I have written to you, fathers, because you know Him who has been from the beginning. I have written to you, young men, because you are strong, and the word of God abides in you, and you have overcome the evil one.

JAMES 4:7–8

7 Submit therefore to God. Resist the devil and he will flee from you.

8 Draw near to God and He will draw near to you. Cleanse your hands, you sinners; and purify your hearts, you double-minded.

• How can you be strong? What habits do you need to adopt to be sure the Word of God is abiding in you?

OBSERVE

Is it possible to walk in complete victory? If so, how?

Leader: Read James 4:7–8 aloud.
> • *Have the group underline **each instruction.***

DISCUSS

• Discuss each instruction. What will be the results of following them?

• Discuss the things that ensure victory in the life of a believer and what that looks like. How can you know that you are standing firm?

WRAP IT UP

Christ has already won the battle. On the cross, almost two thousand years ago, Satan's ultimate defeat was totally assured. He remains a dangerous enemy who wants to destroy you, but his power and authority are limited. God's power, on the other hand, is unlimited and without comparison.

Our prayer is that through this study you have learned the ways of the enemy, that you have seen your responsibility as a believer to stand firm, and that you have discovered how to counter the spiritual attacks that come against every believer. If you would like to explore this subject further, we recommend the study *Lord, Is It Warfare? Teach Me to Stand.*

We pray along with Paul "that the eyes of your heart may be enlightened, so that you will know what is the hope of His calling, what are the riches of the glory of His inheritance in the saints, and what is the surpassing greatness of His power toward us who believe" (Ephesians 1:18–19).

Stay in the Word of God; it is your sword. In the Word you find your strength restored, your love refreshed, and your mind renewed. Then you will sing with King David:

I waited patiently for the LORD;
And He inclined to me and heard my cry.
He brought me up out of the pit of destruction, out of the miry clay,
And He set my feet upon a rock making my footsteps firm.
He put a new song in my mouth, a song of praise to our God;
Many will see and fear
And will trust in the LORD. (Psalm 40:1–3)

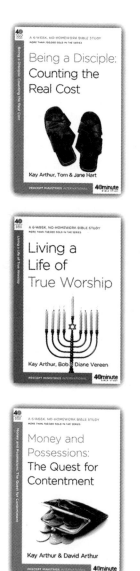
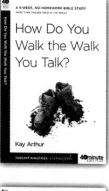
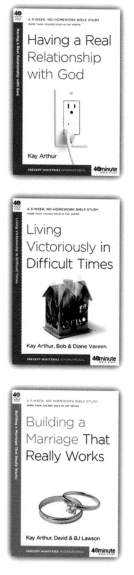
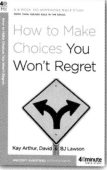
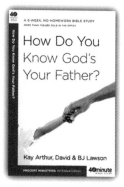

Bible Studies
Discover Truth For Yourself

Also Available:

A Man's Strategy for Conquering Temptation

Rising to the Call of Leadership

Key Principles of Biblical Fasting

What Does the Bible Say About Sex?

Turning Your Heart Toward God

Fatal Distractions: Conquering Destructive Temptations

Spiritual Warfare: Overcoming the Enemy

The Power of Knowing God

Breaking Free from Fear

Another powerful study series
from beloved Bible teacher

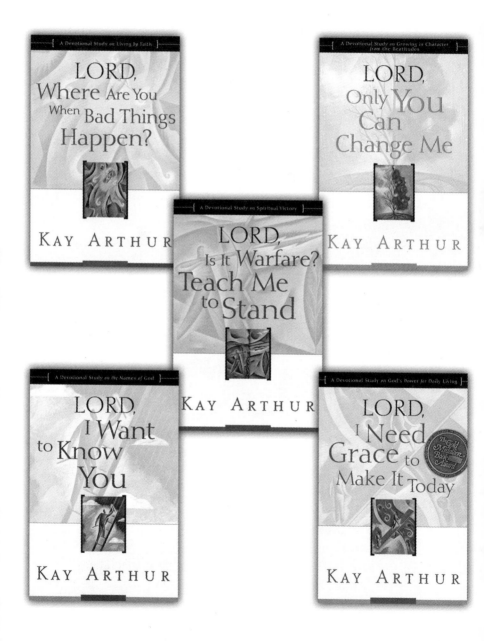

KAY ARTHUR

The Lord series provides insightful, warm-hearted Bible studies designed to meet you where you are—and help you discover God's answers to your deepest needs.

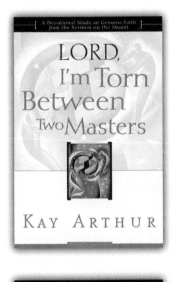

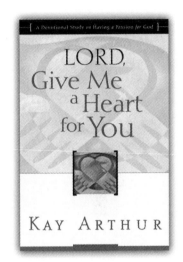

ALSO AVAILABLE:

One-year devotionals to draw you closer to the heart of God.

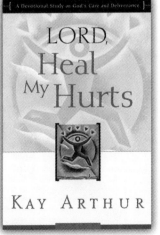

ABOUT KAY ARTHUR AND PRECEPT MINISTRIES INTERNATIONAL

KAY ARTHUR is known around the world as an international Bible teacher, author, conference speaker, and host of the national radio and television programs *Precepts for Life,* which reaches a worldwide viewing audience of over 94 million. A four-time Gold Medallion Award–winning author, Kay has authored more than 100 books and Bible studies.

Kay and her husband, Jack, founded Precept Ministries International in 1970 in Chattanooga, Tennessee, with a vision to establish people in God's Word. Today, the ministry has a worldwide outreach. In addition to inductive study training workshops and thousands of small-group studies across America, PMI reaches nearly 150 countries with inductive Bible studies translated into nearly 70 languages, teaching people to discover Truth for themselves.

Contact Precept Ministries International for more information about inductive Bible studies in your area.

Precept Ministries International
PO Box 182218
Chattanooga, TN 37422-7218
800-763-8280
www.precept.org

ABOUT DAVID AND BJ LAWSON

DAVID AND BJ LAWSON have been involved with Precept Ministries International since 1980. After nine years in the pastorate, they joined PMI full-time as directors of the student ministries and staff teachers and trainers. A featured speaker at PMI conferences and in Precept Upon Precept videos, David writes for the Precept Upon Precept series, the New Inductive Study Series, and the 40-Minute Bible Studies series. BJ has written numerous 40-Minute Bible Studies and serves as the chief editor and developer of the series. In addition she is a featured speaker at PMI women's conferences.